FOREWORD

The historical evolution of Charlestown from a rural medieval backwater to a thriving (and exploitative) industrial hamlet, followed by urban expansion and heavy industry to post-war decline and clearance, is a story seen in numerous places around Greater Manchester. Redevelopment of the 'brownfield' site at Charlestown for housing has allowed archaeologists to examine key elements of the small former industrial hamlet known as Douglas Green, the site of one of Greater Manchester's earliest cotton mills, established in the late 18th century. This lucid and well-illustrated booklet describes investigations of well-preserved remains of the 16th-century hall, farm and outbuildings, and textile manufacturing and processing – set within a local and wider historical context.

CONTENTS

It was pleasing to see the archaeological excavations incorporate opportunities for the local community to take part in the dig. The legacy of the archaeology project includes this popular-style publication as well as an information panel erected on site. This complements similar archaeology outcomes for the Castle Irwell flood defence scheme a short distance to the east. Finds from the dig are deposited with Salford Museum & Art Gallery. All this public engagement work, which has been funded by the developer and delivered by L-P Archaeology and Salford Archaeology, provides a sense of history and place for the existing and incoming new residents of the area in a landscape that today is unrecognisable from its industrial past.

This booklet is number 30 in the *Greater Manchester's Past Revealed* series which seems extraordinary given that the first one, on Piccadilly Place in Manchester, only came out in 2010. Nearly all of these have been funded by developers through planning conditions. They cover a diverse range of below-ground archaeology, historic buildings and places, but many focus on the remarkable industrial heritage of the area. Together, they provide a unique insight into key aspects of Greater Manchester's history, landscape and archaeology.

NORMAN REDHEAD

INTRODUCTION

Charlestown lies close to the south bank of the River Irwell, some 2km to the north-west of Salford city centre. Historically, it was a small settlement in an area known as Brindle Heath, within the semi-rural township of Pendleton. The population of the area began to expand during the post-medieval period, when the local economy was increasingly supplemented by the weaving of textile goods, most notably fustians and linens. Charlestown's location close to the river was also ideally suited to serve the textile-finishing trades such as bleaching, which required an abundance of clean water and open fields. Several bleach crofts were established along the banks of the Irwell during the 18th century, although farming remained essential to the local economy well into the following century.

The mechanisation of the textile industry from the late 18th century onward had an unprecedented impact on society and the economy of the region. The first water-powered mills were strategically placed near strong falls of water to drive their waterwheels. The site of a former corn mill and bleach croft in Charlestown proved to be the perfect location for one of the earliest cotton-spinning mills in the country, which was established by William Douglas in 1781-82. This led to the development of a small industrial colony known as Douglas Green, situated close to the manor house of Pendleton Old Hall.

Industrial expansion throughout the 19th century created a landscape that was characterised by a patchwork of fields interspersed with large factories and tracts of workers' houses to accommodate Pendleton's ever-growing population, who were no doubt drawn to the area by an array of employment opportunities.

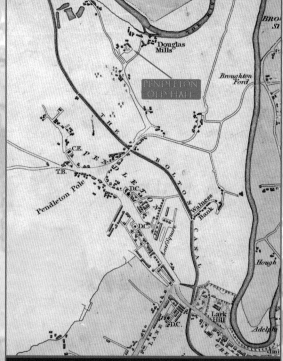

Extract from William Johnson's 'Plan of the Parish of Manchester' of 1820

Aerial photograph of the Charlestown area taken in 1930 looking towards the River Irwell (© Manchester Libraries, Information and Archives)

The origin of Charlestown may be traced to a group of cottages built by Charles Hill in the late 18th century. The hamlet was referred to as 'Charles' Town' as it expanded, eventually becoming known as 'Charlestown'. The settlement had attained its peak of industrial development by the early 20th century, although the Great Depression of the 1920s and 1930s saw a surge in unemployment. To make matters worse, the last of the coal was hauled out of Pendleton Colliery in 1939 and several local textile factories could no longer compete with the price of foreign imports, resulting in population decline. That being said, Irwell Bank Works and the adjacent Suffolk Street Works at Douglas Green continued to provide employment locally until the late 20th century.

Efforts were made to modernise Pendleton's housing stock during the second half of the 20th century, transforming the character of the area. Swathes of Victorian terraces were cleared during the 1960s and replaced with numerous tower blocks and new housing developments, although some of the Victorian terraces survived in Charlestown and Douglas Green, together with dilapidated industrial premises.

Housing redevelopment in Pendleton in the 1960s (© University of Salford)

The 21st century has seen several major regeneration projects brought forward in and around Salford, focusing mainly on providing new homes in densely occupied districts and on redundant industrial sites. One such project by Salford City Council and Keepmoat Homes Ltd has transformed the Charlestown area of Pendleton by providing 425 new homes with shared ownership and affordable rented properties. This major redevelopment scheme, branded Riverbank View at Charlestown, aimed to help tackle the national housing shortage and improve the quality of housing across the area. The project focused on redundant industrial land in Charlestown and Douglas Green, and was delivered in three phases. Not only has the scheme improved an underused part of Pendleton, now offering a brighter future for local and new communities, but it has also provided an exciting opportunity to rediscover Charlestown's rich industrial past.

The boundary of the Riverbank View development area superimposed on a satellite view across Charlestown in 2003 (© Google Earth)

In order to secure archaeological interests in the site, and following the advice of the Greater Manchester Archaeological Advisory Service (GMAAS), Keepmoat Homes Ltd commissioned a desk-top study at an early stage in the design process. This demonstrated that the site had high potential to contain below-ground remains of archaeological interest spanning the post-medieval and industrial periods. In the first instance, a trial trench evaluation was undertaken by L-P Archaeology in 2016. This confirmed that the foundations of historic buildings survived intact as below-ground remains across the Riverbank View site, allowing archaeologists to uncover a range of significant archaeological remains that had a profound impact on the early development of the area. In the light of the findings of the initial trenching, GMAAS recommended that a second stage of more detailed archaeological excavation was carried out in advance of construction work. The first phase comprised an open-area excavation of Pendleton Old Hall and an associated farmhouse, excavated by L-P Archaeology in 2016.

The earliest finds from this excavation can be traced back to before the Dissolution of the Monasteries in the 1530s, when the land at Charlestown was owned by the priory of St Thomas the Martyr in Stafford. Archaeological remains associated with this phase comprised relict soils that contained fragments of 15th- and 16th-century pottery, and some foundations of the post-medieval hall that had occupied the site. Several later phases were also recognised, which mostly comprised the structural remains of Pendleton Old Hall, built in c. 1777. The excavation also exposed below-ground remains of a farmhouse and outbuildings that were still in use in the mid-19th century.

The Riverbank View (Phase 1) site in 2016, during the excavation of Pendleton Old Hall
(© Suave Air Photos)

The excavated remains of the Irwell Bleach Works in 2017 (© Salford Archaeology)

The second and third phases of development were preceded by archaeological excavations of former industrial sites, and were carried out by Salford Archaeology in 2017 and 2020 respectively. The excavation in 2017 targeted the footprint of the cotton mill established in 1781-82 by the infamous William Douglas, whose ill treatment of his workers earned him the nickname 'Black Douglas'. Whilst Douglas' venture was hugely successful, and his mill complex expanded with the addition of more buildings in the late 18th and early 19th centuries, the site was repurposed as the Irwell Bleach Works in the mid-19th century. The majority of the archaeological remains in this area corresponded to this later building, although a few elements of the original cotton mill were exposed.

The third phase of excavation targeted a mid-19th-century cotton mill known as Britannia Mill, which had been converted subsequently to a dye works. The most significant remains to be recorded included the foundations of an early 20th-century chimney, several boiler bases, flues, and the foundation bed for a small engine.

The three sites targeted for excavation during the regeneration scheme give an insight into Charlestown's changing and evolving environs from a rural riverside location into an important industrial and densely occupied settlement. Each excavation has offered a glimpse into slightly different periods of time and helps to capture the development and history of this fascinating area.

The excavated remains of Britannia Mill
(© Salford Archaeology)

Human activity in the area stretches back to at least the Mesolithic period (c. 10,000 – c. 3500 BC), when warmer temperatures and significant environmental changes encouraged people to migrate northwards. Archaeological evidence from the North West implies that early human settlement and other activities took place adjacent to rivers and mossland. The topography of the area suggests that land on the Manchester side of the River Irwell was suitable for early farming as it occupied a comparatively high position on well-drained sands and gravels. Archaeological evidence from Manchester, and especially from the Castlefield area of the city, offers a glimpse into this period through the discovery of stone tools dating from the Mesolithic to the Bronze Age (c. 220 - c. 800 BC).

Mesolithic flint blade foun... during archaeological excavatio... in 2012 near Barton upon Irwe...

Dugout canoe discovered near Barton upon Irwell during the excavation of the Manchester Ship Canal in 1889

Land on the Salford side of the river was low-lying, comprising poorly drained boulder clays that were not conducive for early farming techniques, although a possible prehistoric defensive ditch was excavated on high ground enclosed by a meander in the river at Castle Irwell. The area now occupied by Charlestown, however, would have been unsuitable for early settlers, lying within the floodplain of the River Irwell. Prehistoric activity seems to have been confined to higher ground, to the north of Pendleton, where large scatters of Mesolithic and Neolithic (c. 3500 – c. 2200 BC) material including flint arrowheads have been discovered, although flint scrapers have also been found on Chat Moss and near Barton upon Irwell. The raw material to produce these stone tools was scarce locally and, in comparison to those found elsewhere, the tools are of poor quality.

Other notable artefacts of prehistoric date include a dugout canoe discovered in Barton upon Irwell during construction work for the Manchester Ship Canal in 1889.

Roman occupation of the area commenced in the late 1st century AD and was focused on the fort of *Mamucium* and its extramural settlement or *vicus* in the Castlefield area of Manchester. A network of Roman roads extended from the fort, connecting it to other military posts throughout the region. Salford lay beyond the periphery of the Roman settlement, although the projected course of two Roman roads, one to Wigan and a second heading towards Ribchester, passed through Salford. Some 'native' farmstead sites, such as those discovered at Great Woolden Hall and Port Salford, have produced evidence for Romano-British occupation.

The collapse of Roman administration in the early 5th century was followed by an influx of Germanic and Danish people who settled in various parts of Britain. Evidence of their arrival and their territories can be studied through place-names. Both Pendleton and Pendlebury have early medieval origins, the 'pen' element being derived from the Old English word for 'head' or 'top', and the element 'hyll' meaning hill. The 'ton' suffix is derived from the word for a settlement, 'tun'. Pendleton is likely to have been within the Kingdom of Northumbria before it was conquered by Edward the Elder in the early 10th century and integrated into the Kingdom of Mercia.

A lack of archaeological evidence for this period suggests that Salford was a sparsely populated part of the country. Amongst the few artefacts that have been discovered in the area are the shaft of a Saxon cross found near Eccles church during the construction of the Manchester Ship Canal, and part of a later cross that was discovered at Barton Old Hall. Such crosses were erected near a camp or town by Christian missionaries before preaching. In addition, a cave on Ordsall Lane in Salford is reputed to have been a place of Saxon worship before it became a hermitage for monks of the Cluniac order. The cave was lost to development in the early 19th century.

The Anglo-Saxon kingdoms in England in the 9th century AD

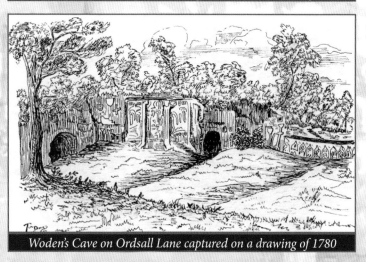

Woden's Cave on Ordsall Lane captured on a drawing of 1780

After the unification of various Anglo-Saxon kingdoms to form the Kingdom of England in AD 927, Salford became a *caput* or royal manor, which was the seat of a large administrative district known as the Hundred of Salford. The hundred contained nine large parishes, including the parish of Eccles, which comprised the five townships of Pendleton, Pendlebury, Clifton, Barton upon Irwell and Worsley. After the Norman Conquest of 1066 the Hundred of Salford was granted to Roger de Poitevin, and at the time of the Domesday Survey of 1086 the area is recorded to have comprised 350 square miles of land, which was mostly forest.

The place-names Pendleton and Pendlebury imply that the two areas were at least occupied by dispersed farmsteads in the early medieval period with a possible fortification in the vicinity. Documents dating to 1168 record monetary transactions, some of which refer to payments for renting land in the Salford Hundred, and also describe the road heading to Pendleton as wide strips of 'waste' where the inhabitants' pigs strayed at will. Other historical evidence implies that an early medieval cross once stood in the vicinity of St Thomas' Church on Broad Street, c. 850m to the south of Douglas Green.

Salford had grown into a sizeable settlement by the beginning of the 13th century and was granted a borough charter in 1228 by Ranulf de Blundeville, the Earl of Chester, followed by a market charter in 1230, permitted by Henry III. The historic core of Salford was centred on the market place and the market cross situated at the junction of Greengate and Gravel Lane.

An early 19th-century lithograph by John Ralston depicting the medieval cross in Salford market place

Agricultural land and pastures surrounded the medieval centre, where produce such as wheat, barley, beans and oats were grown to sell at the weekly market. Although the burgesses were granted many commercial privileges, they were required to grind corn and bake bread at the lord of the manor's corn mill. In 1257, two such corn mills are recorded in Salford, one at Pendleton and a second at Broughton. The location of the Pendleton mill is uncertain, although a likely site is that forming the north-eastern part of Riverbank View. An advertisement for the lease of Pendleton Old Hall noted that there was a disused corn mill on the estate in 1777 powered by an artificial fall of water created by the adjacent weir.

The earliest record of Pendleton appears in a document of 1199 when King John gave 'Pennelton' to Jornechio de Hulton in exchange for Broughton and Kersal. The Norman nobleman Robert de Ferrers inherited the estates in 1260, and the following year he bestowed Pendleton upon the Augustinian priory of St Thomas the Martyr in Stafford. The land owned by the priory was added to in 1332 when Maud de Worsley gave to the prior her land in Pendleton, and, in 1339, Henry the Earl of Lancaster gave the prior 12 acres of heathland in Salford and Pendleton. Pendleton remained in the hands of the priory until the Dissolution of the Monasteries in the 1530s.

By the beginning of the 14th century, Salford was a burgeoning trade centre, dealing primarily in agricultural produce. As the town grew, a greater diversity of trades emerged. In particular, the textile industry began to flourish and played an important role in the local economy by the 16th century. The foundation of the region's textile industry is sometimes credited to an influx of Flemish weavers in the 14th century. Textile processing was undertaken in cottages, comprising the spinning and weaving of traditional fabrics such as wool and linen. Clean atmosphere, stretches of unpolluted water and open fields were required for bleaching and dyeing the textiles. The River Irwell around Pendleton provided an ideal location for these processes to be undertaken.

Ford Maddox Brown's painting, which depicts Queen Philippa greeting Flemish weavers in Manchester in 1363

The Dissolution of the Monasteries, a series of administrative and legal processes implemented between 1536 and 1541 by which Henry VIII disbanded monasteries, priories, convents and friaries in England and Wales, allowed the Crown to expropriate their income and dispose of their assets, and monastic land and buildings were confiscated and sold off to wealthy families. In 1539, as part of this process, land in Pendleton was taken from the priory of St Thomas and granted to Rowland Lee, Bishop of Lichfield. He may have been responsible for building Pendleton Old Hall as a manor house, as it is mentioned in his will. Rowland Lee's property was divided between his four nephews upon his death in 1543, and Pendleton was bequeathed to Bryan Fowler. It was retained by his descendants until the early 18th century, though there is little to suggest that the family resided at Pendleton. The manor passed to the Fitzgerald family in 1733, and remained in their hands until 1912.

Salford expanded during this period, encouraged by the flourishing trade in textile goods, especially woollens. The early Salford Portmote records show the appointment of an overseer 'for measuring cloth' in 1614 and the borough court lists the most important occupations as being mercers, chapmen, weavers, whitsters (bleachers), dyers and cloth workers. The importance of the textile-finishing trades of bleaching and dyeing is implicit on one of the earliest plans of Salford, produced by Joseph Hill in 1740, which marks bleach crofts along the River Irwell as it flows through the heart of the town. Pendleton lies beyond the edge of Hill's map, although it was an ideal location for bleaching, and at least 15 bleachers had settled in the township by the end of the 18th century.

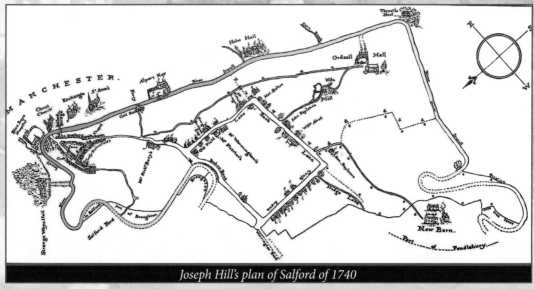

Joseph Hill's plan of Salford of 1740

Traditional Methods Of Bleaching

The quality of finished yarn and cloth was dependent upon the finishing processes and, for it to be printed or dyed successfully, it had to be freed from any impurities by bleaching. This crucial process rendered the material completely white, but the traditional method of bleaching was a lengthy process that could take several months. The first stage, known as 'bucking', was to boil the yarn or cloth in alkaline lye made from wood ashes, followed by a thorough washing in water and steeping in buttermilk. Whitening was then achieved by spreading the material out in the open air, and exposing it to the sun for long periods. This was a seasonal activity, dependent on good weather, and often formed a secondary occupation to farming.

The traditional method of 'bucking' yarn and cloth (reproduced from Barfoot 1840)

Articles printed in 18th-century newspapers provide a flavour of the importance of the bleaching industry in Pendleton. An advert placed in the *Manchester Mercury* in 1762, for instance, states '12 acres of meadow and pasture in the heart of Pendleton at the Pendleton Pole, near to the future site of St Thomas' Church, is to be let by John Gregory with six acres already in use as a fustian bleaching croft'. Another notice printed four years later advertised that 'pot ashes can be ground up at the corn mill at the Old Hall in Pendleton at 9d. per hundred',

A traditional open-air bleach croft

implying that there was an increasing demand locally for alkaline lye for bleaching. A report of several items stolen from a bleach croft in Pendleton was also printed in 1766. These included a 'counterpain, five yards of linen cloth….four bed quilts….half whited, and one sheet'. Further thefts were reported in the 1770s, including printed cotton handkerchiefs that were described as 'light ground with India pattern the whites not clear'.

Pendleton Old Hall

A notice published in a local newspaper in 1777 that advertised the lease of Pendleton Old Hall noted that '....a part of the premises is now occupied as a bleaching croft and would be suitable for a cotton printer'. The lease was taken on by a local textile merchant, William Douglas, who converted the disused corn mill on the estate into one of the first cotton-spinning mills in the country. Douglas demolished the original hall soon after taking up the lease, and had an entirely new manor house and gardens erected on the site.

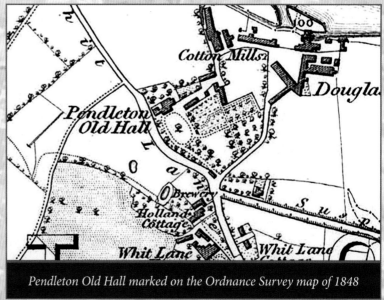

Pendleton Old Hall marked on the Ordnance Survey map of 1848

The development of Riverbank View presented an exciting opportunity to excavate the remains of Pendleton Old Hall in order to learn more about its early development, its layout, and any earlier deposits that may offer an insight into activity on the site during the medieval and post-medieval periods. L-P Archaeology was commissioned by Keepmoat Homes Ltd to undertake the archaeological investigation in 2016, which involved the excavation of two areas. The first trench targeted the site of Pendleton Old Hall, whilst a second trench was placed across the footprint of an adjacent farm building.

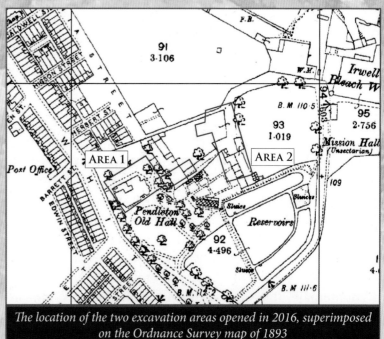

The location of the two excavation areas opened in 2016, superimposed on the Ordnance Survey map of 1893

LATE MEDIEVAL TO LATE 17TH CENTURY

Area 1 exposed archaeological remains deriving from several distinct phases of the development of Pendleton Old Hall. The earliest phase was represented by isolated patches of relict soil that appeared to have developed during the late medieval to early post-medieval periods. These layers contained some interesting fragments of pottery, the earliest of which was part of a handle from a reddish-grey gritty ware vessel with an olive-green glaze. This is likely to have been a large storage vessel, such as a cistern, and has been dated to between the late 14th and 16th centuries. Other early sherds included a handle from a Cistercian ware drinking cup, probably dating to the late 15th or 16th century.

Part of a handle from a late medieval vessel
(© L-P Archaeology)

A group of 17th- and 18th-century pottery fragments was also recovered from the excavation. These included a yellow ware drug jar, black ware and mottled ware drinking tankards, and several slipware bowls, all dating to the late 17th century. This assemblage of fine table wares is typical of material excavated from higher-status post-medieval domestic sites in the North West.

Fragments of a 17th-century slipware dish (left) and a late 17th-century yellow ware jar (right) (© L-P Archaeology)

The earliest structural remains uncovered during the excavation included the foundations of a wall that measured 1.94m long by 0.90m wide with a depth of 0.52m, and consisted of large cut blocks of chiselled red sandstone. The inner core of the wall contained more fragments of pottery and glass dating to the 17th century, whilst a marbled clay tobacco pipe bowl dating from 1620 to 1640 was excavated from the foundation trench, further suggesting a 17th-century construction date. The clay pipe bowl could be Dutch in origin, which gives a tantalising link to the early bleach workers of the area, some of whom are thought to have been Dutch.

Sandstone wall foundations (© L-P Archaeology)

The orientation of the excavated wall foundation was on a slightly different alignment to the hall erected by William Douglas in c. 1777 and is likely to represent the remains of the 16th-century manor house. No further foundations of this early building were identified during the excavation, although the remnants of a cobbled surface exposed to the east of the hall were seemingly associated with the original building. The location of the cobbles and the sandstone foundation suggested that the earlier hall may have been slightly to the north and partially outside the footprint of its late 18th-century successor.

Marbled clay tobacco pipe bowl dated 1620-40 (© L-P Archaeology)

THE LATE 18TH-CENTURY HALL

William Douglas constructed a new hall on the site of the earlier manor house in c. 1777, destroying much of the original building. The archaeological excavation uncovered part of the footprint of this late 18th-century hall, including a cellar in the south-west corner. The cellar measured 5.8m by 3.7m and was paved with large sandstone flags that covered a grid of brick and slate culverts, which would have provided drainage.

Features identified within the cellar included the remains of a mullioned window in the south-east corner, and a load-bearing brick structure, possibly for a chimney situated to the north of the window. The elevation on the western side of the window was altered and once housed the original entrance into the room via a staircase. At the northern elevation was a later entrance with a short corridor leading to a staircase. Other modifications included the addition of buttresses to strengthen the bowing walls of the cellar.

The cellar in the south-west corner of the hall (© L-P Archaeology)

Aerial view of the excavated remains of Pendleton Old Hall exposed in Area 1 (© Suave Air Photos)

A notice printed in the *Manchester Courier* in 1834 advertising the lease of Pendleton Old Hall contained a detailed description of the interior rooms and the extent of the estate:

'The house comprises dining room 24 feet by 17 feet, drawing room 34 feet by 18 feet and breakfast room 18 feet by 15 feet, two kitchens with sculleries and other conveniences on the ground floor, 13 lodging rooms with closets or dressing rooms the whole forming a desirable residence for one large family or two small families, the house being so constructed as to make at pleasure, two distinctive dwellings together with the garden and pleasure grounds (containing about four acres) well stocked with choice of fruit and ornamental trees, hot house and green house, both furnished with vines and plants of the choicest sorts and in full vigour. There is also about 56 acres of meadow land belonging to the above premises, in a high state of cultivation, with shipponing for 24 cows, stabling for nine horses, coach house, entrance lodge and a cottage in the yard for the farmer.'

The lease of Pendleton Old Hall was advertised for let again in 1841, together with William Douglas' cotton mill. By 1848, the mill had been converted for use as a bleach works by Thomas Holmes & Sons, who also took on the hall. An extension was added to the north-east corner of the hall in the mid-19th century, represented by two large brick-built cellars. The easternmost cellar measured 10m long by 5.46m wide and was paved with bricks. Surviving features included a small cold store set in the northern elevation, together with a sloped tiled chute for delivering goods.

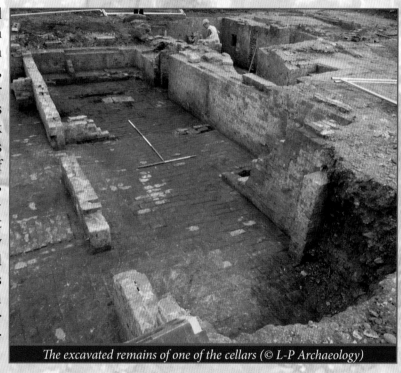
The excavated remains of one of the cellars (© L-P Archaeology)

The adjacent cellar measured 10m long by 3m wide and provided a space for coal storage and washing facilities, and is likely to have been frequented by domestic servants. Some internal fixtures provided evidence of the installation of gas pipes and a communication system, presumably used by servants to receive instructions from upstairs.

The original entrance into the cellar appeared to have been via the staircase that ran off a corridor in the earliest room, although access to this staircase had been blocked subsequently. The remains of a replacement staircase were uncovered in the north-west corner of the cellar. The south-west cellar was also modified during this period, following the construction of the new wing. This included blocking the doorway between the adjacent rooms and the insertion of a corridor with a quarter-turn staircase.

Pendleton Old Hall provided a home for several different owners of the bleach works during the second half of the 19th century, but it was unoccupied by 1891. The building was converted subsequently for use as a public reading room, which necessitated the addition of a toilet block. The entire building was finally demolished in 1918.

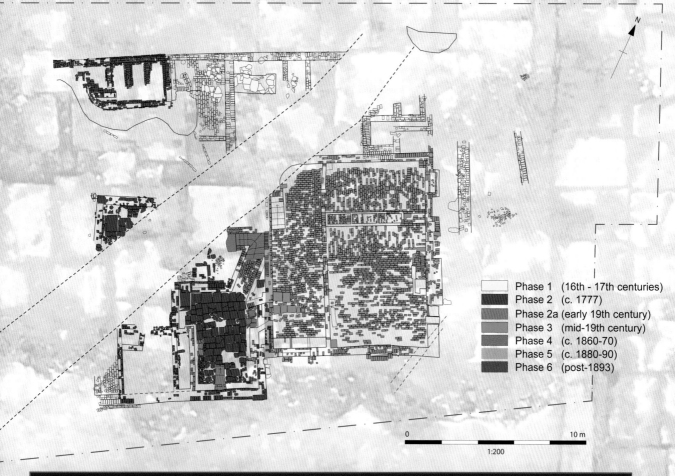

Phase 1	(16th - 17th centuries)
Phase 2	(c. 1777)
Phase 2a	(early 19th century)
Phase 3	(mid-19th century)
Phase 4	(c. 1860-70)
Phase 5	(c. 1880-90)
Phase 6	(post-1893)

0   10 m

1:200

Plan of the excavated remains of Pendleton Old Hall (© L-P Archaeology)

EARLY COTTON MILLS

The mechanisation of the textile industry in the 18th century led to profound social and economic changes. The first successful textile mill was designed for silk throwing, and was established on the River Derwent in Derby by Thomas Lombe in 1720. At five storeys high, 33.5m long and 12m wide, with the machinery powered by a waterwheel, Lombe's silk mill set the standard for the multi-storey cotton and woollen mills that had become prevalent along rivers across England by the end of the 18th century.

Thomas Lombe's silk mill on the River Derwent in Derby provided a model for the first generation of water-powered cotton mills in the late 18th century

The mechanisation of the cotton industry began in the mid-18th century with a series of inventions by Lancashire-based entrepreneurs. Central to these was a machine patented by Richard Arkwright in 1769 that was capable of spinning cotton yarn. This became known as the water frame once Arkwright had adapted the machine so that it could be powered by a waterwheel.

The success of the water frame allowed Arkwright to attract the financial backing required to employ the machine on a commercial basis, and led him and his financial partners to build a large cotton mill at Cromford in Derbyshire in 1771. This five-storey mill, powered by a large waterwheel, became the world's first successful cotton-spinning mill.

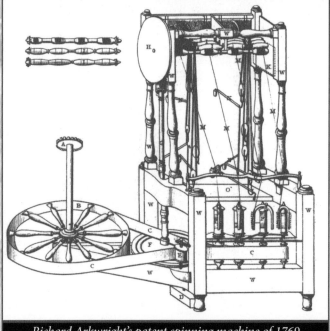

Richard Arkwright's patent spinning machine of 1769

Spinning was only one stage in the process of producing cotton yarn, and the tasks required to prepare the raw cotton for spinning were still carried out by hand. In 1775, however, Arkwright made significant improvements to a carding machine invented by Lewis Paul in 1748, and patented a machine that successfully converted raw cotton into a cotton lap that was suitable for spinning. The introduction of this rotary carding engine enabled the entire process of producing spun yarn from raw cotton to be mechanised, signalling the birth of the modern factory system. In the words of one historian, the success achieved by Arkwright 'resounded through the land, and capitalists flocked to him to buy his patent machines or permission to use them', and numerous water-powered cotton mills were established using Arkwright's patent machinery.

Carding engines captured on a coloured lithograph by James Barfoot in 1840

The waterwheel technology of the 18th century was better suited to relatively small rivers and streams flowing swiftly, and appropriate sites were often to be found in relatively narrow valleys in the countryside. The major watercourses in Manchester and Salford, however, are broad and sluggish and offered very few appropriate sites for water-powered mills. A rapid survey of Arkwright-type mills in Britain carried out in 1788 recorded just four water-powered mills in Manchester and Salford. Those recorded on the River Irwell in Salford were Douglas Mill in Pendleton and Bank Mill below The Crescent, which were both set to work in 1781-82.

An illustration printed in Bradshaw's Manchester Journal of 1841 featuring Bank Mill on the River Irwell, viewed from The Crescent in Salford

William Douglas and Douglas' Cotton Mills

Douglas' mill was one of the earliest, if not the first, cotton factory in the Salford area, and was certainly the largest. It was established by William Douglas, the son and seventh child of John Douglas, an innkeeper on Hyde Park Road in London. William was despatched to Manchester at a young age to gain experience of business and, by the early 1770s, he was trading as a fustian manufacturer based in St Ann's Square in Manchester.

With the financial backing of his elder brother Thomas, William Douglas obtained the lease of Pendleton Old Hall and the adjacent corn mill in 1777. The mill had fallen into disrepair in the 1760s, and its equipment was advertised for sale in 1768. It is referred to as 'disused' in a slightly later newspaper notice, which advertised the lease of Pendleton Old Hall.

Upon securing the lease of the hall and its estate, William Douglas set about reconstructing the redundant corn mill as a cotton mill. He installed Arkwright-style water frames to spin the cotton yarn, which was then sold to cloth merchants for distribution to handloom weavers. The mill had set to work by February 1782 and by the end of the decade had become one of the largest cotton mills in the whole of the Manchester district, with between 3000 and 4000 spindles at work.

To be LETT, Together or in Parcels,

And Entered upon at Candlemas next,

A MESSUAGE, with the Appurtenances, called the OLD HALL, in *Pendleton*, within 2½ Statute Miles of *Manchester* Market Place, and containing upwards of twenty Acres of good Meadow, Arable and Pasture Land, of the large *Cheshire* Measure, of eight Yards to the Pole. The River *Irwell* runs thro' the Land, and there is a constant Supply of Spring Water from the rising Grounds adjoining.

There is a CORN MILL on the Estate, which is now disused, on Account of the Weir being down.— A Part of the Premises is now occupied as a Bleaching Croft, and would be very suitable for a Cotton Printer, &c. The Buildings are good, and a Tenant may be accommodated with any new ones, and with any other Conveniencies that the Situation will admit of.

Further Particulars may be had by applying to Mr. *Hugh Oldham*, at *Strangeways* Hall, or his Chambers, side of the Shambles, *Manchester*, where a Plan of the Premises may be seen.

An advertisement printed in the Manchester Mercury *in January 1777*

A water frame displayed in Helmshore Textile Museum

William Douglas earned a notorious reputation for the pitiless treatment of the pauper apprentices employed as cheap labour in his cotton mill, and was often referred to as 'Black Douglas'. It is estimated that Douglas hired around 150 parish or pauper apprentices, mostly from London, from the age of six-years old upwards. The apprentices endured long hours of hard toil in dangerous working conditions in exchange for basic food, clothes and accommodation. Some committed suicide, and those who survived their apprenticeship were often so deformed that the mill became

Notice printed in a local newspaper in July 1791

known as the 'Cripple Factory' or the 'White Slave Mill'. A flavour of the harsh treatment of mill workers is implicit in the Quarter Session rolls for 1783, which record that George Wood was sent to prison for six weeks for 'absenting himself from the service of his masters, William and Thomas Douglas'. In the same year, Martha Fleet was found guilty of stealing four hanks of cotton worth sixpence and was sentenced to a public whipping.

Numerous notices in the *Manchester Mercury* record apprentices absconding from Douglas' mill, presumably on account of their severe mistreatment. One such notice, dated February 1785, advised that William Douglas would take legal action against any person who gave employment to nine 'servants' that had been articled to work in his mill but 'have left their respective services against the consent of their masters'. The 'servants' in question included four teenage boys, aged between 14 and 19, together with Elizabeth Willson and her four children.

Cartoon by Robert Cruikshank (1832), depicting brutality to pauper apprentices in a cotton mill

EXCAVATING DOUGLAS' MILL

The original mill was six storeys high with a cellar and an attic, measured approximately 30m long and 8m wide, and was powered by a huge waterwheel that was rated at 70 horsepower. This is shown on historic mapping to have been supplied with water via a short but wide millrace that was built just above a weir across the River Irwell. This weir had probably served the corn mill originally, but had to be reconstructed by William Douglas when he took the lease of the site. The weir had to be rebuilt again in 1786 following extensive damage caused by a surge of floodwaters.

Most of the footprint of the mill lay within the northern part of the Riverbank View development area, and was subject to excavation by Salford Archaeology in 2016. This open-area trench was centred on the footprint of William Douglas' mill of 1781-82 and the part of the Irwell Bleach Works that superseded the mill in the mid-19th century. The clearance and redevelopment of the site following a devastating fire in 1850, however, meant that few archaeological remains of Douglas' mill survived intact, although excavated elements of a millrace almost certainly dated to the late 18th century.

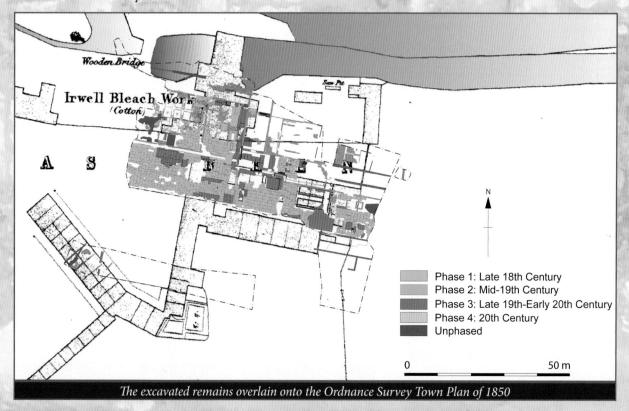

Phase 1: Late 18th Century
Phase 2: Mid-19th Century
Phase 3: Late 19th-Early 20th Century
Phase 4: 20th Century
Unphased

0   50 m

The excavated remains overlain onto the Ordnance Survey Town Plan of 1850

A wall constructed of hand-made bricks, revealed along the north-western part of the excavation area and lying parallel to the River Irwell, had formed the southern wall of this millrace. This lay to the south of the main headrace for the waterwheel, and may have been a continuation of a much narrower millrace shown on 19th-century maps.

The millrace survived for a distance of at least 14m, beyond which it had been remodelled for use in the bleach works. The majority of the original wall was excavated to a maximum depth of 0.7m, although limited excavation of one section revealed the base of the channel at a depth just over 3m below the modern ground surface.

Curved southern wall of the millrace during excavation
(© Salford Archaeology)

The millrace had a barrel-vaulted capping as it continued beneath the floor of the bleach works towards the tailrace marked on Ordnance Survey mapping. Excavation to a depth in excess of 4.5m below the modern ground surface failed to reveal the base of the tailrace, but did uncover a thick deposit of waterlogged silt.

The base of the vaulted capping during excavation
(© Salford Archaeology)

Organic material in the tailrace
(© Salford Archaeology)

THE SECOND COTTON MILL

The application of steam power to the textile industry in the final years of the 18th century meant that mills were no longer restricted to a riverside location, leading to the birth of the urban textile mill. This was especially important in Salford and Manchester where there were limited opportunities to utilise water power, and led to the rapid ascendancy of the Manchester district as the world's leading centre for the factory-based cotton industry.

Keeping up with the latest technology, William Douglas became the first cotton spinner in the Salford area to employ a steam engine. This 12 horsepower engine was supplied by Boulton & Watt of Birmingham, the leading manufacturers of steam engines, and was used to drive a second mill that Douglas added to his complex in 1792. The new mill was four storeys high, with a cellar, and was shorter but slightly wider than the original mill, with outbuildings that included cotton mixing rooms, warping and winding rooms, a warehouse, waste room, smithy, and a joiners' shop.

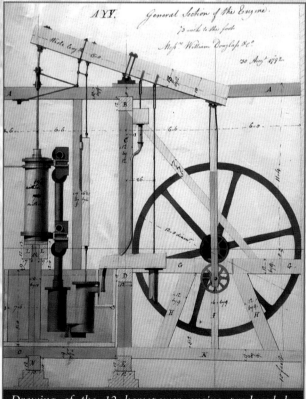

Drawing of the 12 horsepower engine produced by Boulton & Watt for William Douglas in 1792

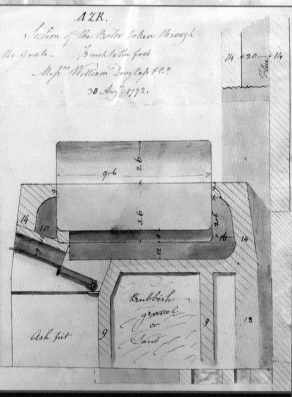

Boulton & Watt drawing of the boiler they supplied with the steam engine in 1792

The new mill was evidently designed to house spinning mules in addition to the Arkwright-type water frames. The spinning mule, a hand-powered machine invented by Samuel Crompton in 1779, was capable of spinning much finer cotton thread than was possible on a water frame. Improvements to the design of the mule in the early 1790s rendered the machine much larger and, crucially, enabled it to be powered mechanically.

In January 1803, William Douglas placed an advertisement in local newspapers that sought 'water and mule spinners with their own piecers', adding that 'there are now ready fitted up on the mill premises for the reception of families, several spacious cottages, built last summer'.

William Douglas died in January 1810, and the business was taken over by his son, John Douglas. It seems that John did not have his father's interest in the textile industry, and instead focused his attention on banking. The cotton mills were evidently struggling by 1841 as the machinery was advertised for sale and, by 1847, both mills had been taken over by Thomas Holmes & Sons and converted for use as a bleach works. In December 1850, however, the original mill was completely destroyed by fire, although the huge waterwheel survived intact. It seems that the second cotton mill was also cleared in the aftermath of the fire, and the entire site redeveloped as the Irwell Bleach Works.

A spinning mule built by John Kennedy in Manchester in the early 1790s. Kennedy is reputed to have been the first to apply steam power to a spinning mule

Spinning mules captured on a coloured lithograph by James Barfoot in 1840. Note the child collecting cotton waste beneath the moving machinery

THE HOUSES

In addition to the two cotton mills, ancillary buildings and an accommodation block for the apprentices, William Douglas also built houses for his other employees as a means of attracting a workforce. In doing so, he effectively created the industrial settlement, or colony, of Douglas Green, which comprised the mills, workers' houses, a shop and a mission hall with seats for 100 worshippers.

The Ordnance Survey Town Plan of 1850 is the earliest map to show the individual buildings at Douglas Green in any detail, although only the eastern part of the settlement was covered by the survey. This plan shows a block of 20 back-

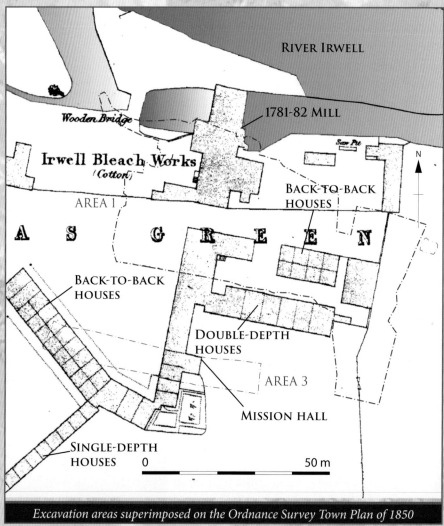

Excavation areas superimposed on the Ordnance Survey Town Plan of 1850

to-back houses and a row of nine single-depth cottages to the south-west of the original mill, with another block of eight back-to-backs to the south-east, together with a parallel row of six double-depth houses. According to a newspaper article printed in 1841, however, there were 48 two-storey cottages, together with 12 three-storey dwellings, whilst the census returns for the same year record 84 inhabited houses at Douglas Green, and 28 that were unoccupied. All of these dwellings had been demolished by the 1890s, with the exception of six double-depth houses and the mission hall, which survived until the 1920s.

A sample of the workers' houses was targeted for excavation in 2017, but it became rapidly apparent that nearly all of the foundations had been removed during demolition. The surviving remains were limited to small patches of internal brick-built floors of two of the back-to-backs and traces of wall foundation trenches.

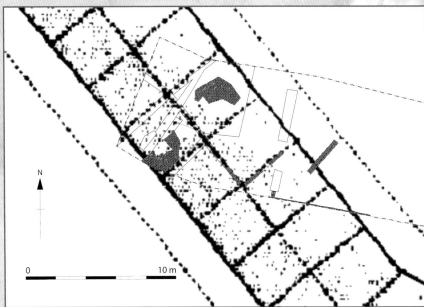

The excavated remains of the back-to-back houses superimposed onto the Ordnance Survey Town Plan of 1850 (© Salford Archaeology)

Despite the lack of surviving remains, it was evident that the footprint of each back-to-back measured 3.6m by 3.5m, providing a ground-floor living space of just 12.6m². Whilst small, the size of these rooms was slightly larger than some workers' houses of a similar date that have been excavated in Manchester and Salford city centres, especially in the poorer districts such as Ancoats. In addition, the surviving wall stubs were one brick length wide, implying that the dwellings were better built in comparison with those in the town centres, which were often divided by just a single skin of bricks.

The remains of brick floors inside the back-to-back houses (© Salford Archaeology)

Douglas' mill remained the only cotton factory in Pendleton until 1797, when Taylor, Weston & Co started a mill beyond Broad Street, 1.2km to the south of Douglas Green. Houses in what became the Ellor Street district were gradually built around the new mill, and the first streets of Charlestown, situated between the two cotton mills, also developed as one of the earliest working-class districts of Salford. There was no settlement nucleus in the township at the start of the 19th century, although a centre was beginning to develop at Pendleton Pole, a triangular green with a maypole, overlooking the junction of the roads from Manchester to Eccles and Bolton. This became recognised as the centre of Pendleton after 1831 when the impressive St Thomas' Church was built to replace an earlier church of the same name of *c.* 1777; this church was renamed St Anne's.

Despite these developments and a growing population, Pendleton retained a rural character well into the 19th century, with a landscape dominated by enclosed fields and scattered farmsteads. Amongst these was a farmstead adjacent to Pendleton Old Hall, which is likely to have been the 'messuage with outbuildings and 20 acres of land' that was advertised in 1753 following the death of John Whittle, the tenant farmer. He was described as a dairy farmer with five cows, two mares, a gelding, a cart and two fully equipped butteries. The farm had been cleared by the mid-20th century but its foundations were excavated by L-P Archaeology in 2016, providing a window into rural living amidst a busy industrial area with close connections to Pendleton Old Hall and Douglas' mill.

Aerial view of the farm during excavation (© Suave Air Photos)

Cobbled bank and timber-lined drain (© L-P Archaeology)

The central part of the excavation area was dominated by a cobbled yard that had formed the main approach to the farm, and extended as a roadway leading north towards Douglas' mills. Historical mapping shows that the cobbled yard also continued to the west, providing access to the grounds of Pendleton Old Hall.

The earliest feature to be found during the excavation was a stone-built drain lined with wooden planks. This was uncovered adjacent to the roadway leading to Douglas' mills and was associated with a cobbled bank, which had seemingly been built to funnel surface water into the drain. The scale of this drainage system was beyond that required for domestic purposes and it may perhaps have been associated with an 18th-century bleach croft.

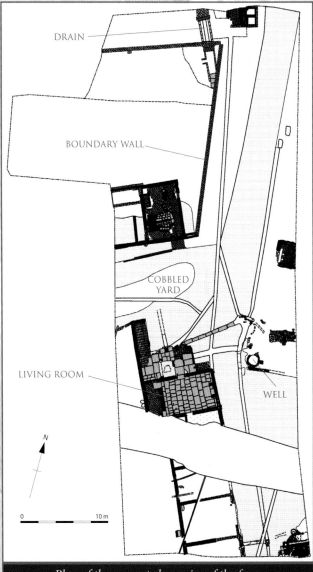
Plan of the excavated remains of the farm
(© L-P Archaeology)

The drain underwent a series of modifications in the 19th century, including the addition of an arched brick capping to create a culvert. This extended beneath a substantial stone wall that formed the boundary of the grounds to Pendleton Old Hall. The culverting of the drain enabled it to be built over.

The foundations of the farm building were uncovered in the southern part of the excavation area, and showed evidence for several phases of modifications consistent with its use up to the mid-20th century. The northern end of the building range had formed the living area, and comprised a single room that measured 5.9m by 3.95m and was surfaced with flagstones. A brick floor along the western side of the living room formed a corridor or entrance vestibule. The southern parts of the building had almost certainly been used to house livestock, and may also have incorporated a dairy and a barn.

The living room at the northern end of the farm building (© L-P Archaeology)

Amongst the finds recovered from the excavation of the farm building were several fragments of clay tobacco pipes that dated to the 19th century. These included a pipe bowl that was stamped 'DUBLIN', which was either made in Ireland or produced for the Irish community in Salford. A large assemblage of 19th-century pottery was also recovered from the farm, including fragments of transfer-printed pearlware and mocha ware plates and bowls, together with numerous utilitarian earthenware storage jars and part of a Lancashire & Yorkshire Railway cup.

The foundations of an outbuilding were revealed on the northern side of the farmyard. This had been built over an earlier structure of which only fragmentary foundations survived. It wasn't possible to determine the size of this earlier building, or whether it had formed part of the farm. Another outbuilding to the east of the farmhouse also appears on the Ordnance Survey map of 1893. Archaeological remains of this structure survived as a brick floor along the edge of the excavation. Beneath the floor was a drainage system that fed into the main stone-built culvert.

The brick floor of the outbuilding on the north side of the farmyard (© L-P Archaeology)

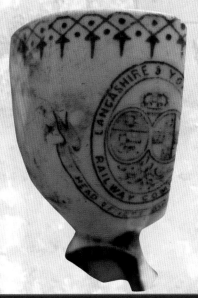

Fragment of a cup (© L-P Archaeology)

The well during excavation (© L-P Archaeology)

A well set into the cobbled yard was uncovered to the north-east of the farmhouse. This had a diameter of 1.45m, and extended to a depth of approximately 6m. It was constructed of a single skin of hand-made bricks with no apparent mortar bond. The well is likely to have been sunk when the farm was built, and remained in use until the 20th century.

Further evidence for farming at the site came from the discovery of two small rectangular pits that lay to the east of the cobbled yard. These contained the remains of pig skeletons, one of which appeared to have been articulated and had no cut marks indicative of butchery. This might imply that the animal was diseased and was buried outside the farmyard. The second pig burial had been disturbed by later activity.

0   1 m

One of the excavated pig burials (© L-P Archaeology)

INDUSTRIAL GROWTH

TRANSPORT IMPROVEMENTS

Industrial expansion was dependent upon several factors, including good transport connections. Pendleton lay at a fork in the main road leading north-westwards from Salford, with one branch leading to Eccles and the other to Bolton. This junction is marked as Pendleton Green on a map surveyed by John Ogilby and printed in his *Britannia* of 1675, the first road atlas of Britain.

The routes to Eccles and Bolton surveyed by Ogilby are likely to have been more akin to tracks rather than roads in the modern sense of the word, although both came under the control of the Pendleton District Turnpike Trust in the 1750s and will have been upgraded at that date. A toll was charged to travel along a turnpike road and the revenue was used for maintenance. Toll bars were built across both roads at the junction at Pendleton Green, separated by the Woolpack Inn that served travellers from at least 1786.

Extract from John Ogilby's 'Britannia'

Painting of the Manchester, Bolton & Bury Canal at Pendleton by E. Hutchinson, showing Pendleton Colliery in the background (Salford Museum & Art Gallery)

The next significant improvement to the local transport network was the Manchester, Bolton & Bury Canal, which opened by 1797. It ran for 17 miles from its terminus basin in Salford to Prestolee, where it crossed the River Irwell and then divided into branches to Bolton and Bury.

The Manchester, Bolton & Bury Canal Company converted into a railway company and opened the Manchester to Bolton railway in 1831. This connected Salford to Manchester and Bolton, and passed through Pendleton. The line was taken over by the Manchester & Leeds Railway in 1846, which became the Lancashire & Yorkshire Railway in 1847, as shown on the Ordnance Survey map of 1848.

Coal

The earliest textile works in Pendleton were built on the banks of the River Irwell, where water was readily available for power and processing. With the introduction of the steam engine, new factories were increasingly built close to sources of coal and transport. The coal seams at Pendleton and Agecroft began to play a prominent role in the local economy in the early 19th century, with collieries supplying coal to industry. Initially the coal was transported via the canal, which prompted the building of a group of cotton mills near the canal terminus on Oldfield Road in Salford.

Pendleton Colliery lay within the Pendleton estate that was still in the hands of the Fitzgerald family. John Purcell Fitzgerald sunk shafts into the coal seams to the north-west of Douglas Green in the late 1820s. The first shaft had reached a depth of nearly 200m by 1832, and nearly 27,000 tons of coal had been extracted within the first six months, although the shaft was abandoned in 1834 due to flooding of the underground workings.

In 1835, Fitzgerald formed the Pendleton Colliery Company with George Stephenson, a renowned civil and mechanical engineer who is best known for his work on the railways. Stephenson supervised the sinking of two deep shafts in 1836-37, and whilst a steam engine was installed to help pump out water the mine did not generate the revenue that had been predicted due to persistent water ingress. Further flooding in 1843 caused the pit to be closed, at a time when the mine employed 1000 people and produced 1000 tons of coal a day.

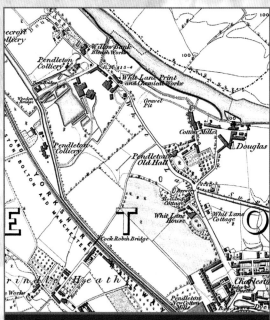

Extract from the Ordnance Survey map of 1848 showing the two collieries and the route of the canal and railway through Pendleton

A view of Pendleton Colliery published in the Illustrated London News *in October 1877*

After several disasters relating to flooding Fitzgerald filed for bankruptcy in 1848, and the mineral rights were bought by Andrew Knowles & Son in 1852. New shafts were sunk in 1857, eventually reaching a depth of 1097m, making Pendleton the deepest colliery in Britain. The colliery became part of the Manchester Collieries in 1929, and finally closed in 1939.

Factory Based Bleaching and Dyeing

A massive growth in the demand for cotton goods from the late 18th century required the processes of bleaching and dyeing cloth to become more efficient to keep pace with the major improvements in other branches of the textile industry. Charles Tennant achieved a significant breakthrough in 1798 by impregnating dry-slaked lime with chlorine gas to create a bleaching powder. This, together with the introduction of powered machinery, led to the widespread adoption of the factory system and the transferral of the bleaching process from the traditional crofts in fields to indoors. Bleaching became a continuous process that was carried out in specialised factories, some of which also had dyeing departments to impart a range of colour to the bleached yarn and cloth.

Once delivered to a bleach works, it became standard practice after the 1830s to sew numerous lengths, or pieces, of the cloth together to form a continuous rope of cloth that could be up to 12km long. This allowed it to be hauled between the various bleaching processes by winches, which drew the rope of cloth through overhead porcelain eyes. From the sewing rooms, the rope of cloth was transferred to the bleach croft for processing. The bleach croft was the largest area within a bleach works, and contained many items of machinery, including steam engines, washing machines, liming machines, high-pressure kiers and cisterns.

The interior of a bleach croft in the early 20th century, showing the rope of cloth passing between the different stages in the bleaching process

The initial processes carried out in the bleach croft were known as the 'grey wash', where the cloth was soaked in a souring liquor to break down oils and grease, washed in water and then dried by squeezing through rollers. Large cylinders known as dash wheels were used in the early 19th century to wash bundles of cloth, although these began to be superseded in the 1830s by a machine that could wash lengths of cloth sewn together into a continuous rope.

Dash wheels at Thomas Hoyle's bleach works in Dukinfield captured on a print of 1843

The washed cloth was then boiled in a lime solution for several hours in a large cylinder known as a kier to completely remove any residual waxy coating on the cloth. It was then passed through a washing machine to remove all the lime solution in readiness for the next stage in the process, referred to as the 'grey sour'. This involved treating the cloth with a weak solution of hydrochloric acid to dissolve any traces of lime and other insoluble soaps. It was then washed again and transferred to another kier for boiling in soda ash.

A final thorough rinse in a washing machine left the cloth ready for actual bleaching, or chemicing, which was achieved by saturating the cloth in a solution of bleaching powder. After allowing the chemical reactions to take place, the last step was to pass the cloth through a dilute solution of sulphuric acid, a stage known as the 'white sour'. This was followed immediately by a final washing in clean water, which rendered the cloth perfectly pure and ready to be dyed or printed.

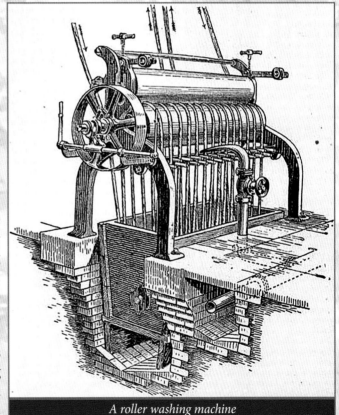

A roller washing machine

The dyes used in all branches of the textile industry until the mid-19th century were natural, and came mainly from plants, animals and minerals. Indigo, madder and logwood were the main sources and were used extensively in Europe in the 18th century. Indigo is a plant native to India and other Asian countries and forms a blue dye, whilst a red colourant was obtained from the roots of the madder plant, imported mainly from the Middle East. Logwood is extracted from the heartwood of logwood trees, and was imported from Central America to produce violet, grey and black dyes.

(L - R): Processed indigo, logwood dyed sample fabrics, madder dyed sample fabrics

The simplest way of dyeing was by mixing a colouring agent with water in a vat and placing cloth in the dye bath to allow the fibres to absorb the colour. Some natural colouring matter, however, could not be made into dyes easily, or did not adhere to the cloth well. These problems were solved by the introduction of chemically produced dyes in the mid-19th century, which cost less and ultimately offered a huge range of new colours.

Factory based dyeing captured in a lithograph of 1840

William Henry Perkin

The first synthetic dye was discovered in 1856 by William Henry Perkin, an 18-year old student at the Royal College of Chemistry in London who had been assigned to carry out a series of experiments to see if it was possible to synthesise quinine, an expensive natural substance that was needed to treat malaria. Whilst carrying out further experiments in his apartment during the Easter vacation, Perkin accidentally discovered that a rich purple dye could be produced by reacting aniline with potassium dichromate, and then extracting the dye by adding alcohol. He set up his own company to produce 'mauve aniline', heralding the birth of a new industry that was to be of great benefit to the textile-finishing trades.

Silk dress dyed with mauve aniline dye

Google honoured Sir William Henry Perkin on his 180th birthday with a doodle (© Google)

Synthetic dye rapidly became the height of fashion and was especially popular with socially mobile and upper-class women, whilst the brightness of mauve aniline also attracted radical and artistically inclined dressers who wanted to be noticed. It was also popular with Queen Victoria, who is known to have worn a mauve dress to the International Exhibition of 1862 and at numerous official engagements during the following decades. The immediate success of mauve aniline paved the way for the introduction of a range of synthetic dyes that became easily available at a comparatively low cost to the textile-finishing industry.

Queen Victoria at her Golden Jubilee in 1887, wearing a mauve aniline dress

Douglas' mills were taken over by Thomas Holmes & Sons in the mid-1840s and converted for use as a bleach works. Whilst textile-finishing works typically comprised an assortment of one- and two-storey buildings, Holmes took the unusual approach of adapting a six-storey cotton mill for bleaching. It was described in 1850 as 'one of our largest bleach works, filled with machinery and gearing of a very complete and expensive description'. The first floor contained mangles and calendering machines, with damping and stretching frames on the second floor. The third, fourth and fifth floors, however, were removed to create a single lofty apartment for drying the bleached cloth. This was heated by hot air from fires that was conveyed by pipes through the various rooms.

It was in the drying room that a serious fire started in December 1850, creating a blaze that could be seen easily from Salford, from where two fire engines set off to Douglas Green without waiting for an official summons. The entire building was enveloped in a mass of flames and part of the roof had collapsed by the time the fire engines arrived, and the blaze was not extinguished for another four hours. The only part of the six-storey mill to survive intact was the massive waterwheel, together with the adjacent bleaching shed and packing room. The estimated cost of the damage was £6,000, but this did not deter Thomas Holmes from building a new bleach works immediately after the fire.

Aerial view of Charlestown and Douglas Green in 1930, showing the Irwell Bleach Works in the background (© Manchester Libraries, Information and Archives)

Thomas Holmes & Sons remained in business until the early 1870s, when the Irwell Bleach Works was taken over by James Barrett. He died within a few years and the works passed to John Walton, a bleacher and dyer. The works suffered another fire in 1883, which damaged goods to the value of £6,000. Despite this set-back, John Walton remained at the Irwell Bleach Works until the early 1940s, although it had been repurposed as the Irwell Bank Works by the early 1950s, and was given over to producing oil seals. The large Suffolk Street Works, another textile-finishing factory, had also been erected to the south of the Irwell Bank Works by the early 1950s.

Aerial view of the Irwell Bank Works taken in 1988, shortly before its demolition (courtesy of GMAAS)

The Irwell Bank Works was demolished in the late 20th century, although the well-preserved foundations of the buildings were uncovered by Salford Archaeology in 2017 during the second phase of archaeological works at Riverbank View. The archaeological remains mainly correspond to the footprint of the rebuilt bleach works shown on the Ordnance Survey Town Plan of 1890, and included a large part of the bleach croft, the foundation beds for numerous machines and steam engines, and a series of stone-built tanks or vats and associated drains beneath the factory floor.

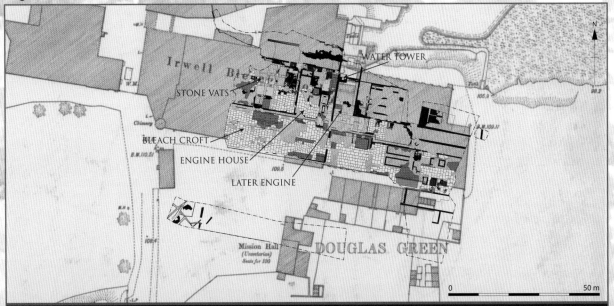

The excavated remains superimposed on the Ordnance Survey Town Plan of 1890 (© Salford Archaeology)

The excavation uncovered a series of large rooms within the works. The most extensive of these was in excess of 35m long and 12.5m wide and had probably been the bleach croft where the main bleaching processes were carried out.

The bleach croft lay in the south-western part of the excavated area, and comprised a flagstone floor into which were set several rectangular machine bases and foundation beds for small steam engines, aligned in two parallel rows. The largest of these was nearly 6m long and 0.8m wide, and was pierced by a series of circular holes. These will have housed vertical iron rods used for holding a large machine in position.

A narrow passage along the north side of the bleach croft is likely to have been a gearing alley. This will have contained a drive shaft from the main steam engine, which will have provided power to some of the machinery via bevel gears and line shafts.

View across the flagstone floor of the bleach croft, showing a series of vats in the adjacent room (© Salford Archaeology)

One of the stone machine bases set into the flagstone floor of the bleach croft (© Salford Archaeology)

A smaller room immediately to the north of the gearing alley contained the well-preserved remains of at least eight stone-built vats that were set into the flagstone floor. Each vat measured between 2.5m and 2.8m long, 2.2m wide and between 0.91m and 1.03m deep, with stone sides that were 0.3m thick. The stone base of some of the vats retained a drain, allowing liquid to be discharged into the River Irwell via a series of drains.

The vats were arranged in a grid, with a 0.7m wide walkway between each. The interior of some of the vats was stained greenish-yellow or yellowish-orange, suggesting that they may have been used for dyeing the cloth. A network of iron pipes connected to the vats implied that they had been steam heated.

High-level view of the stone vats (© Salford Archaeology)

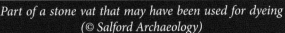
Part of a stone vat that may have been used for dyeing (© Salford Archaeology)

One of the stone vats, showing the brick walkway around the edge (© Salford Archaeology)

Excavation of a room in the centre of the bleach works, adjacent to that containing the stone vats and between the bleach croft and the millrace for the waterwheel, revealed a series of substantial stone blocks that had formed the foundation beds for a large steam engine. Each of the stone blocks measured just over 6m long by 2.4m wide and 0.75m thick, and retained iron rods that had held the engine in place. This internal engine house lay across the width of the building, and will have been the main source of power for the machinery in the bleach works, although the excavation demonstrated that it had been supplemented by several smaller engines.

It seems that the waterwheel also continued to provide power to the bleach works, at least during its first years of operation. Several features deriving from the power-transmission system from the waterwheel were uncovered during the excavation, including several large stone blocks and cast-iron bearing boxes that were set into the wall of the millrace. These appear to have been associated with a huge iron casting that will have housed bevel gears to transfer power from the drive shaft connected to the waterwheel to different parts of the works.

Foundation beds for the main steam engine
(© Salford Archaeology)

Iron casting that housed the transmission gearing
(© Salford Archaeology)

The excavation provided evidence for internal alterations to the bleach works during the late 19th and early 20th centuries, represented by the use of machine-made bricks bonded with a very dark grey mortar and concrete. Some of these alterations may have been required in the light of the findings of the Mersey & Irwell Joint Committee in 1894, which demanded that numerous textile-finishing firms, including the Irwell Bleach Works, purified the effluent from their works before it was discharged into the River Irwell. This probably led to the construction of a series of filter beds to the west of the bleach works, which are first shown on the Ordnance Survey map of 1908.

Changes were also made to the power systems during the late 19th century with the installation of new steam engines. The largest of these was represented by a row of substantial stone blocks that were uncovered immediately to the south-east of the earlier engine in the centre of the bleach works.

Foundation beds for a replacement steam engine (© Salford Archaeology)

Another interesting element of the Irwell Bleach Works that was uncovered during the excavation was a square base for a water tower. This measured 2.4m by 2.4m and contained a large stone block and the vestiges of a mechanism that ran vertically from the base.

The use of water towers for pressurised water systems developed during the mid-19th century, and they were often operated in conjunction with reservoirs that stored water close to where it would be used. Water towers were designed to supply water via gravity as the water was stored in an elevated tank. A source of power was required to pump water up to the tank once it had been emptied, a function that may have been addressed at the Irwell Bleach Works by the steam engine that occupied the foundation beds adjacent to the tower.

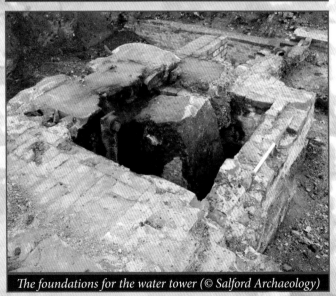

The foundations for the water tower (© Salford Archaeology)

Agricultural land on the bank of the River Irwell a short distance to the north-west of Irwell Bleach Works was developed as an integrated cotton spinning and weaving mill in the mid-19th century. Known as Britannia Mills, this new cotton factory was established by William Cottrill & Co, most likely in 1853, although some historical records suggest that the mill was in production as early as 1848. The mills rapidly gained a reputation as a 'state-of-the-art' factory, housing 25,000 spindles and 620 looms, providing employment for 700 people. Trade directories of the period describe the products of the mill as either 'fancy' or 'coloured'.

William Cottrill was a well-known local industrialist during his lifetime. He became heavily involved in Manchester politics and served twice as a councillor, once as an alderman and was apparently invited to be mayor of Salford, a position that he declined. He was also a member of the influential Manchester Chamber of Commerce.

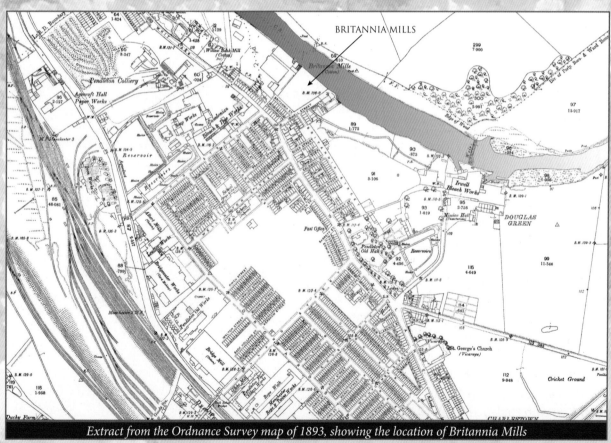

Extract from the Ordnance Survey map of 1893, showing the location of Britannia Mills

William Cottrill is perhaps best known, however, for his impressive art collection and for his relationship with the French impressionist Edgar Degas, whose well-known work, *A Cotton Office in New Orleans*, is reputed to have been intended originally for Cottrill although it was eventually sold to the Municipal Museum in Pau, France.

Cottrill regularly displayed works of art at the Royal Manchester Institution and other galleries but, in 1873, he was compelled to sell his collection of 81 watercolours and 161 oil paintings, together with his large villa residence in Higher Broughton, to raise an injection of capital for his business and keep Britannia Mills in operation. As with many cotton manufacturers in Lancashire, Cottrill & Co sustained a huge financial loss during the Lancashire Cotton Famine of the 1860s and the severe economic depression that characterised the 1870s.

William Cottrill died in 1891 and Britannia Mills were taken over by his sons John and Harry Cottrill, although they appear to have relocated the family business to mills in Kearsley and Farnworth by the end of the 19th century. Britannia Mills was sold to Samuel Ashton & Co and repurposed as the Britannia Dye Works. This continued in operation for several decades but most of the buildings were demolished in 1949-53 and new industrial premises erected in their place.

A Cotton Office in New Orleans, painted by Edgar Degas in 1873

Britannia Dye Works in 1949, shortly before demolition

The site of Britannia Mills lay within the third phase of the Riverbank View development and was subject to an archaeological investigation in 2020. Whilst some of the buildings' foundations had been removed completely in the 20th century, the remains of a boiler house and its associated flues and chimney were uncovered, together with a large section of the factory floor.

The excavation provided evidence for the development and layout of the 19th-century cotton mill, and its later use as a dye works. Whilst the sequence of historic maps shows the configuration of the various mill buildings, little was known about their internal arrangement.

Aerial view of the excavated remains of Britannia Mills
(© Salford Archaeology)

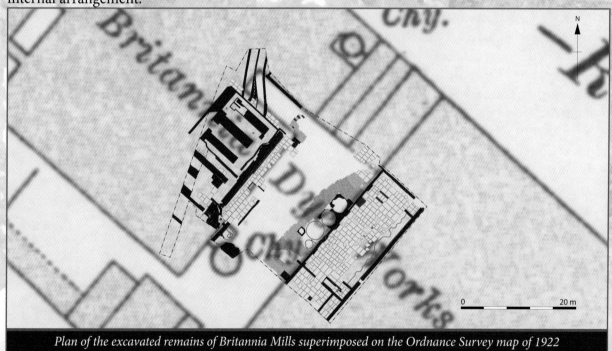

Plan of the excavated remains of Britannia Mills superimposed on the Ordnance Survey map of 1922
(© Salford Archaeology)

Most of the foundations exposed in the south-eastern part of the excavation area dated to the original construction of the Britannia Mills in c. 1853. These included the brick-built external walls of one of the mill buildings and an intact flagstone floor. The stone-built foundations for what was probably the original boiler house on the north side of the central yard were also uncovered, although this building had been reconstructed completely in the early 20th century.

The rebuilt boiler house appeared to have been open-fronted on its south-eastern side, overlooking the central yard, from where the boilers will have been charged with coal. The roof of the building was supported by rows of cast-iron columns, the remains of which were uncovered between the boiler bays.

The boiler house had been designed to contain three Lancashire boilers, each measuring just over 8m in length, with a common flue situated to the rear.

The excavated remains of Britannia Mills (© Salford Archaeology)

The excavated remains of the central boiler bay, showing the characteristic T-shaped setting for the twin flues at the rear (© Salford Archaeology)

The flue to the rear of the boilers carried the exhaust gases to a new chimney that was erected in the mill yard in the early 20th century. The flue was lined with refractory bricks to withstand the heat of the exhaust gases, whilst the external walls were constructed of common brick.

Promotional illustration of an economiser

The flue split into two on its approach to the chimney, with the main branch entering a rectangular chamber. Much of this structure lay beyond the edge of the excavated area, although sufficient was revealed to allow its identification as the base for an economiser.

This device consisted of banks of cast-iron pipes, usually 0.1m in diameter and 2.75m long, that were set into the flue. The feed water to the boilers passed through the bank of pipes, which were heated by the hot exhaust gases making their way from the boilers to the chimney. An economiser could increase the temperature of feed water for the boilers from about 65°C to 120°C, thereby offering a considerable saving in the amount of coal required to produce steam.

The remains of the economiser and the bypass flue
(© Salford Archaeology)

A section of the main flue at the rear of the boiler house
(© Salford Archaeology)

The second branch of the flue acted as a bypass, and was fitted with a large iron baffle that controlled the amount of hot gases that could be drawn through instead of passing into the economiser. The two branches reconnected before entering the chimney.

Part of the chimney in the mill yard was uncovered during the excavation. The base was constructed of machine-pressed bricks, with the outer wall measuring 1.2m thick. The inner face of the chimney was lined with refractory bricks, similar to those used in the flue.

The latest remains uncovered during the excavation included the bases for three large circular tanks that were probably added to the site in the late 1920s as part of the dyeing process.

The excavated remains of the chimney base (© Salford Archaeology)

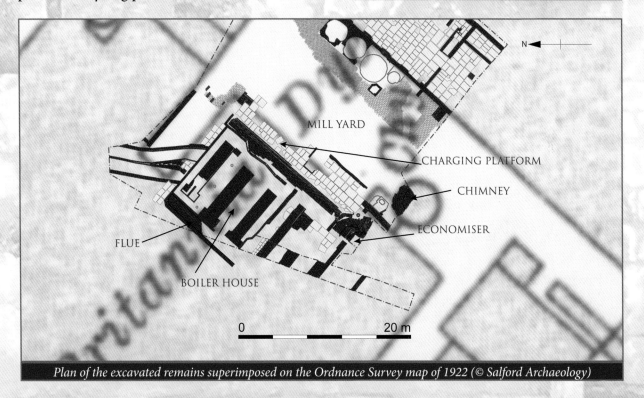

Plan of the excavated remains superimposed on the Ordnance Survey map of 1922 (© Salford Archaeology)

Industrial development along the southern bank of the River Irwell had attracted increasing numbers of workers to the area by the turn of the 20th century. Whit Lane had been developed almost entirely by 1890, with residential properties extending from the course of the road. Land between Whit Lane and the Lancashire & Yorkshire railway line had also been infilled by housing, together with industrial premises directly adjacent to the railway. Pendleton Old Hall was acquired by the Salford Corporation in 1893 and was repurposed as a public reading room, whilst the gardens were turned into public recreation areas that included a bowling green.

Pendleton Old Hall following its conversion for use as public reading rooms. This closed in 1918, and the building was demolished shortly afterwards

More rows of terraced housing had been erected to the east of Irwell Bleach Works by 1920, and a new, large factory known as the Suffolk Street Works was built to the south. Some of the industries that had long provided occupations for the population of Pendleton, however, began to fail in the wake of the Great Depression of the 1920s and 1930s. Pendleton Colliery, for instance, closed in 1939, and most of the buildings associated with Britannia Dye Works were cleared in 1947-53.

A major programme of housing renewal was implemented across Salford in the mid-1950s, and the redevelopment of Pendleton began with large-scale clearance. New housing legislation required designated space and large open areas between buildings, although this policy meant that only a small proportion of the local population could be accommodated on the same area. This raised the prospect of the local authority losing revenue due to a reduction in the number of ratepayers, which was a factor in Salford Borough Council deciding to pursue high-rise solutions. The first three 15-storey residential towers in Pendleton, known as the John Lester, Walter Greenwood and Eddie Coleman blocks, were erected in 1962.

The first three residential towers to be built in Pendleton in the early 1960s (© University of Salford)

Amidst some concern over standards and lack of civic amenities, the government encouraged Salford Borough Council to appoint Robert Matthew and Percy Johnson-Marshall as 'architect planners' to manage the design and delivery of the next phases of redevelopment. Matthew had previously served as the Chief Architect for London County Council, where he gained repute for his pioneering role in social housing. The plan was to create what was described at the time as 'a Salford of the Space Age'-a modern, pedestrianised, high-density, residential area that was free of industry but had tree-lined open spaces, a community centre and a health centre, accompanied by a new civic and administrative centre and a multi-level regional shopping centre with the capacity to park up to 2,000 cars.

'A Salford of the Space Age': Pendleton in the 1970s
(© University of Salford)

The new residential towers were generally well received by local residents in the 1970s, although the proposed civic centre did not materialise and the shopping centre failed to become a regional hub. Indications that the comprehensive redevelopment of the area was failing in social and economic terms, however, were becoming apparent by the late 1980s, with Charlestown in particular suffering from issues of high levels of deprivation, low population density, poor housing and high rates of unemployment.

The University of Salford's Peel Building (1896) in front of several late 20th-century tower blocks

The shopping precinct with the residential Briar Hill Court tower to the rear

The pressing need for new regeneration initiatives was clearly evident by the early 21st century, and it was also recognised that a new approach was required. A key strand in the regeneration of Pendleton was the ambitious Riverbank View development. Keepmoat Homes Ltd was selected as Salford City Council's preferred development partner for the scheme, which obtained planning consent in 2016 to redevelop 14.39 hectares of land in Charlestown for 425 new homes with associated landscaping and public open space to include a new play area, a

Riverbank View development proposal plan

football pitch and a waterside cycle and pedestrian route. Following consultation with the Greater Manchester Archaeological Advisory Service (GMAAS), a condition was attached to planning consent that required a scheme of archaeological works to be implemented.

GMAAS' recommendation to carry out an archaeological investigation in advance of construction work was in line with the protocols set out in the National Planning Policy Framework (NPPF), which advises that the importance of known or suspected archaeological sites should be assessed where they are threatened by development, and that any remains should be protected, either through sympathetic planning or, where appropriate, through archaeological excavation and recording.

Salford City councillors and planners viewing the remains of Pendleton Old Hall (© GMAAS)

Volunteers from the local community participating in the excavation of Pendleton Old Hall in 2016 (© GMAAS)

Volunteers from the local community participating in the excavation of Pendleton Old Hall in 2016 (© GMAAS)

As part of the archaeological works, volunteers from the local community were given the opportunity to work on site as part of a programme of public outreach, which included organised school visits, site tours, information boards and evening public lectures.

It was also a requirement of the planning condition that the results obtained from the archaeological investigation of Douglas Green were disseminated to the public in an appropriate format. It has been the intention of this booklet to help fulfil this requirement, and present an illustrated summary of the findings from the archaeological excavations of this historically significant area, and celebrate the rich heritage of Pendleton.

The booklet has been produced in tandem with the preparation of several information panels. These are to be installed as part of the landscaping works associated with the Riverbank View development, and are intended to share the fascinating story of Douglas Green with new residents.

TIMELINE

1257	Record mentions a water-powered corn mill in Pendleton
1261	Robert de Ferrers bestowed Pendleton upon the Augustinian priory of St. Thomas the Martyr
1540s	Pendleton Old Hall built by Rowland Lee
1771	Richard Arkwright established the world's first successful cotton-spinning mill in Cromford, Derbyshire
c. 1777	Pendleton Old Hall dismantled and reconstructed by William Douglas as an entirely new manor house
1781-82	William Douglas established his cotton mill and the factory settlement of Douglas Green
1797	Manchester, Bolton & Bury Canal opened
1798	Charles Tennant introduced bleaching powder
1810	Death of William Douglas
1831	Manchester & Bolton Railway opened
1835	Pendleton Colliery Company formed
1850	Douglas' mill destroyed by fire shortly after being repurposed as a bleach works
c. 1853	William Cottrill & Co established Britannia Mills in Charlestown
1856	First synthetic dye discovered by William Henry Perkin
1861-65	Lancashire Cotton Famine
1894	Mersey & Irwell Joint Committee directed textile-finishing works to purify their effluent prior to discharging into the rivers
1918	Pendleton Old Hall demolished
1939	Pendleton Colliery closed
1986	Irwell Bank Works demolished

BLEACH CROFT
a piece of land or building where bleaching is carried out.

CARDING ENGINE
a machine that disentangled and combed textile fibres mechanically into lengths, preparing them for spinning.

CALENDAR
a series of pressure rollers used to form or smooth a sheet of material.

DASH WHEELS
large hollow wheels divided into compartments that were filled with bundles of cloth and water. Impurities were washed out of the cloth as the dash wheel was spun rapidly.

FINISHING
after cloth has been woven, it goes through a series of finishing processes, which can include bleaching, dyeing and printing.

FUSTIAN
a strong, twilled cloth, with a linen warp and a cotton weft, although the term is also used to describe a variety of heavy woven cloth prepared for menswear. The production of fustian increased steadily in the Manchester area during the early 17th century.

HEADRACE
a channel that feeds water to a mill or waterwheel.

KIER
a large cylindrical boiler or vat used in bleaching or scouring cotton cloth.

PANCHEON
a large, flaring, shallow earthenware bowl commonly used in rural communities.

PIECER
an operative employed by a mule spinner to tie together strands of cotton which broke whilst spinning. This job was usually undertaken by children.

TAILRACE
a channel that conveys water away from a waterwheel after use.

FURTHER READING

- C. Aspin, 2003 *The Water Spinners*, Helmshore

- J.R. Barfoot, 1840 *The Progress of Cotton*, London

- R.L. Greenall, 2000 *The Making of Victorian Salford*, Lancaster

- K. Honeyman, 2007 Child Workers in England, 1780-1820, London

- I. Miller, 2012 *An Industrial Art: The Archaeology of Calico Printing in the Irwell Valley*, Greater Manchester's Past Revealed, 6, Lancaster

- I. Miller and C. Wild, 2015 *Hell Upon Earth: The Archaeology of Angel Meadow*, Greater Manchester's Past Revealed, 14, Lancaster

- R. Reader, 2018 *Castle Irwell: A Meander Through Time*, Greater Manchester's Past Revealed, 22, Salford

- *ecclesoldroad.co.uk*

Excavating the remains of Pendleton Old Hall in 2016 (© L-P Archaeology)

Riverbank View during development in 2017 (© Keepmoat Homes Ltd.)

The detailed excavation reports, together with the project archives, have been deposited with the Salford Museum & Art Gallery in Salford. Copies of the reports have also been lodged with the Greater Manchester Historic Environment Record, maintained by GMAAS at the University of Salford.

Publications in the *Greater Manchester's Past Revealed* series are available from GMAAS and digital copies can be downloaded at https://gmaas.salford.ac.uk/publications/